GOD
IN THE 21ST CENTURY

UNIVERSAL SPIRITUAL
AWARENESS

Other Books by the Author:

The Numinous Factor

Finding God in the Quantum

GOD
IN THE 21ST CENTURY

UNIVERSAL SPIRITUAL AWARENESS

John L. Walker, Ph.D.

Park Point
PRESS

Park Point Press is an imprint of Centers for Spiritual Living
573 Park Point Drive | Golden CO 80401

God in the 21st Century: Universal Spiritual Awareness
Copyright © 2022, John L. Walker

All rights reserved.
No part of this book may be reproduced in any form without permission in writing from the publisher, except for brief quotations embodied in critical articles or reviews.

Park Point Press
573 Park Point Drive
Golden, CO 80401-7402
720-496-1370

www.csl.org/publications/books
www.scienceofmind.com/publish-your-book

Printed in the United States of America
Published May 2022

Editor: Julie Mierau, JM Wordsmith
Design/Layout: Maria Robinson, Designs On You, LLC

ISBN paperback: 978-1-956198-17-1
ISBN ebook: 978-1-956198-18-8

PRAISE FOR

God in the 21st Century

John Walker's book **God in the 21st Century** launches the reader into a fairly easy entry point of the "Omnis." John then takes the reader through energy, vibrations, the quantum field, and personification, bringing the journeyer home with a sense of Universal Spiritual Awareness.

— *AUTHOR REV. CHRISTIAN SØRENSEN, D.D.*

God in the 21st Century: Universal Spiritual Awareness explains the science of God or creative intelligence in a way that everyone can understand. The energy behind "all that is" begins to make sense. While I may not understand the entire field of quantum physics, I get an understanding of what is unseen in the world. A must read for anyone who wants to know about how energy operates.

— *REV. DEBBIE MCDONNELL*

To Corky

My Joy & Inspiration

Table of Contents

Dedication		vii
ch1	What	1
ch2	Om³	13
ch3	Energy	27
ch4	Vibrations & Frequencies	41
ch5	The Quantum	53
ch6	Personification	63
ch7	Universal Spiritual Awareness	77
About the Author		83
Bibliography		85

GOD
IN THE 21ST CENTURY

UNIVERSAL SPIRITUAL AWARENESS

CHAPTER 1

WHAT

God is what?!? You must be kidding!

No, this is not a kidding matter. It is time here in the 21st century to lift our understanding of God to a higher level than that of ancient peoples who had limited spiritual and worldly awareness. The keys to understanding Infinite God have been with us all along, but limited knowledge has kept humans from grasping them.

For instance, some in olden days thought that the Earth was flat and the sky just a dome overhead, beyond which God sat on a golden throne judging people just like a tribal chieftain or local king would, since that was all the government they knew. Our knowledge of the Earth, the universe, and society now far surpasses the level of those ancients, but for many, the concept of God still has not changed much.

This book offers glimpses of some completely new concepts for us to ponder in our meditations and in our dealings with others. It will endeavor not to state facts but, rather, to give suggestions on how we might bring our awareness of God, of the universe, and of the functioning of our higher minds to a new level of spirituality for the good of ourselves and of humanity.

Let us look around at a hypothetical audience at a concert hall during an operatic performance. One person is sound asleep. Another is drowsy, only partly aware of what is going on. Another is turned off, obviously unimpressed, even annoyed, by the whole thing. Another seems lost in other thoughts, only checking in occasionally. Another has a puzzled look, not able to understand much of it. Another is watching and listening intently, eyes darting about as if analyzing everything logically. Another, armed with a book on musical appreciation, is understanding and liking the show. And another is identifying so much with the performance as to be caught up in a sublime, almost spiritual, bliss.

The word "consciousness" relates to awareness, and we see that the members of the audience show varying levels of consciousness. They are, in order: unconsciousness, semi-consciousness, denial, distraction, limited understanding, pure rationality, positive mind set, and spiritual sensation. There is no criticism in this; people just are, and need to be accepted at whatever level they choose to be on.

But contemplation may show that we can see these same levels of awareness in peoples' approach to God: they may be totally unaware of the nature or presence of God; only partly aware; somewhat aware but uninterested; somewhat aware but distracted; somewhat aware but unable to understand; mildly enjoying the experience; or caught up in a spiritual euphoria.

Since the member of the audience getting the most from the performance might seem to be the one most aware of its total beauty, we can suspect that the best way to "worship" God is to become aware, completely aware, of the total presence of God in a limitless, absorbing way. Opening our personal awarenesses in this way is called "enlightenment," and may be the most important thing we do in this life.

This handbook offers some points to ponder that we can consider applying toward this opening of our higher minds to getting and appreciating a greater view of God than we might now have. It is not a strictly rational approach, although the universe itself is mostly rational, but it will bring us up to the 21st century level of scientific thought that can open our minds to up-to-date intuitive insight, since neither God nor, as we will find out, the universe can be understood through logic alone. In fact, some of the physical laws of the universe seem to be set up in such a way as to prohibit our understanding their operations at all. But God still operates.

So we now have the scientist who derives truth from the facts of logic and experimentation, and the mystic who derives truth from intuition, imagination, and direct revelation. It is time to combine the two into one.

Let's consider shedding some of our old, self-imposed limitations that actually block a higher view of the universe and of spirituality. As human beings, we are accustomed to thinking and operating within limits. We remember that Einstein was considered brilliant, not only for his abilities as a physicist, but also for his expansive imagination that allowed him to inquire and picture what might happen if things did this or that. When our unlimited imaginations soar, we can see much more from their new heights. We will, therefore, look at some suggestions that can expand our thinking, and we will then contemplate ways of using these to open our minds to greater spiritual awareness through intuition, another name for direct revelation.

To distinguish the new, expanded, unlimited view of God from the typical limited views from historical religions that people carry with them and accept without thinking, we will use the symbol ∞, or infinity, for the former, so that "∞ God" would be read as "Infinite God" or "Infinity God."

This is because new information and insights arise so rapidly these days that trying to use old ideas and terms by putting patches on them and pretending they are new is of little effect. We need to take a quantum leap, as it is called, into major changes and new truths. This is much like how an earthquake often occurs. A fault line can have two adjacent masses trying to slip past each other, but friction holds them up. They keep straining and stretching, slipping an inch here and there, until they suddenly snap and there is a massive movement.

Likewise, we humans can move from an old, scientific concept of a limited, observed, material universe to an interactive, thoughtful, spiritual one where waves of possibilities resolve in myriad ways, not just into the obvious one, and objects are energy fields rather than just things, all of which we will see evidence of here. Thus, many of our old, narrow, religious ideas must be released from their limitations to be relevant today.

To illustrate how we will do this, picture a science classroom in which the teacher puts six new wooden pencils of the same length on the table and challenges the students to make four equilateral triangles with them.

Naturally, they lay out three to make one triangle, then use the common side and two more to make a second, but then are stumped with only one pencil left to make the last two. The teacher points out that they are visualizing in only two dimensions and need to think outside the box. The teacher then takes the first triangle and lays the other three pencils across it to make the other three triangles. They are of different sizes, of course, but are all equilateral.

The students may protest that they thought the triangles all had to be the same size. The teacher agrees with that and challenges them to do it that way. Again they fail, even though they try to do it in three dimensions, such as piling up three pencils on one side, which doesn't work because they don't stay and are not touching the main triangle anyway. The teacher then starts with the basic three pencils in a triangle on the table, takes the other three and, holding them together at their points, puts the eraser ends at each of the points on the flat triangle, thus making three more tall triangles with the sides of all four the same length. The teacher gently points out that the students needed to think even farther out of the box to solve the second challenge.

So now we need to think much farther outside the box than we may be accustomed to doing with the task before us. Let's start thinking without limits right now.

Ancient people could deal with God in local terms because they lived in limited societies, often out of touch with each other. All they could see were the simple things around them. So God would be seen as a chieftain leading His people into battle against other people; rewarding some while punishing others; requiring worship, cajoling, and sacrifices; making mistakes and repenting of them; and needing the help of others in fighting His battles as a local deity might do.

We, however, are in the 21st century. We know the Earth is not flat, but is a globe hanging in the vastness of space. We know the sky is actually that vastness of space. We know of the great complexity and enormous forces of the subatomic world, held in check with exact precision. We know of the intricacy of the human body, with its cellular system, and brain. We know of the billions of galaxies in the universe and realize we are not the center of everything.

We see how our Earth is starting to interact with the solar system, such as through manned lunar landings, Mars rovers with humans getting ready to follow them, and rockets to the edge of our farthest planets. We know that the basic building materials of our human bodies, such as carbon and oxygen, came to this Earth from distant stars. It is impossible for us to deal with a deity of just this Earth.

Instead, we can open our awarenesses to an infinite God, or ∞ God, that is not just of this Earth, not just of our solar system, not just of our galaxy, but is of the vastness of the universe, the great All That Is. We can realize the impossibility of puny human intelligence trying to set limits on ∞ God or on deciding where ∞ God's boundaries are or where ∞ God's influence stops and some other influence starts. Let us decide right now to consider ∞ God without any human-imposed limits to see where this freedom takes us.

The one thing that will not be discussed here, however, is that fatal question: Why? There is no way we can presume to know the mind of ∞ God. We will just look at universal phenomena and try to expand our spirituality to greater awareness of ∞ God that way.

The book is short for a purpose: It can be read quickly to get an overview in one complete picture. But it does need to be read in sequence because the picture unfolds logically, with each section depending on what has gone before. Skipping around gives fragmented pieces out of order, and we will have to admit that ∞ God does seem to use logic and orderliness throughout the universe, so we should do the same.

Let us ponder a basic thought: The only way to understand something thoroughly and completely is to *be* it, and to *know* that we are it.

Otherwise, we only know *about* it. This could mean ∞ God really *is* all the things in the universe in order to know all of them totally.

We can start to see this by looking closely at three words that have often been used to describe Deity over the years. These have been understood in limited ways, as we will soon see. We need to open our awarenesses to what they *really* mean.

The words are: Omniscient, Omnipotent, and Omnipresent. We can refer to them collectively as Om^3.

Bringing the Awareness into Focus for Chapter 1

- There are many levels of consciousness, with some more focused and aware than others, thus enabling some people to see and understand more clearly than others.
- The rapid growth of knowledge and insights in today's world highlights the need to shed old limitations in favor of new spiritual realities and dimensions.
- It might be convenient to use the term "∞ God" or "Infinite God" or "Infinity God" to designate a newer, unlimited concept of Deity.

CHAPTER 2

Om³

In mathematical terms, Om³ means Om multiplied by itself, then multiplied by itself again, meaning that its effects build on each other and are much greater than if the terms were just added together. So these three characteristics, which have been used throughout the generations to describe ∞God, multiply and interact with each other to an astonishing degree when used in an unlimited sense.

OMNISCIENT

Omniscient means "all-knowing," and when used to describe Deity, refers to how ∞ God must know everything in order to be responsible for every aspect of the universe. In fact, reflection may show ∞ God to be the Author of all knowledge or else something could exist before ∞ God knew of it, which would be an impossibility. It is vital that ∞ God be infinite in knowledge.

As an example, we humans, only recently on the scene, keep discovering more and more about electricity, but ∞ God had to know everything about it throughout all time for the universe to be as it is.

Omniscience is huge and complex. The word includes knowing all facts relating to everything throughout the universe, whether in material form or not, from the operations of billions of galaxies to the complexities of a subatomic world so small we humans can barely comprehend it.

Omniscience also involves keeping track of all matter in all its stages of development, of all anti-matter, and of all the vast amounts of dark matter throughout the universe that humans do not, as yet, comprehend. And it means knowing all thoughts and mental images that have ever been had by any and all living, thinking beings on this planet or on any other, which is a staggering complexity in itself.

Does this sound like too much? We are just getting started.

Omniscience goes even farther than this enormous view. It is worth pondering that there can be no human thought that is not actually of ∞ God in the first place. There does not seem to be any physical evidence that our brains actually create thoughts. They just sort and classify and use them. Our creative minds almost seem to be separate from our brains, with separate energy supplies.

In fact, there is evidence that consciousness can continue after the brain itself is considered dead, so conscious thought again seems to be separate from the brain. Since brains seem able to repeat or even analyze thoughts, but not originate them, each thought might be seen as part and parcel of the Infinite.

When people try to find their Supreme Being, they miss the point that the very thoughts by which they are searching could be of the spiritual realm itself. And, since every action starts as a thought, all actions could also be of ∞ God. Then, since emotions are linked to thoughts, all emotions might also be of ∞God. It is worth pondering.

There might be two aspects of ∞God to consider: that which makes up everything, and that which gives the spark of life to some things, much like how a tree is of ∞God but may or may not have the spark of life at any particular time.

So thoughts and emotions can be both of ∞God and generated by ∞God. This can be a new and extraordinary concept for some people, but it will become clearer and more evident when we consider Omnipresence, wherein ∞God may be sensed as being everywhere, in and as everything.

A fish, so far as we know, does not have the concept of water because he is in it. It is his medium of life and he does not even know it is there. (Given the five-second attention span of a fish, he would quickly forget it anyway.) Likewise, we humans may be living in a medium, an atmosphere, a life-giving source that is ∞God, but we do not see or sense it. Instead, we go around looking for it as being separate from us when we may be in it all the time. So, again, quite possibly, ∞God is all there is, and includes our thinking, sensing, and perceiving this.

Thus, we must be careful not to apply our judgments of good or evil to the things of ∞God. These words imply opinions based on limited human perception and varied circumstances. Killing a person might be considered bad in one set of circumstances but good in another or both good and bad, depending on differing human opinions, which themselves might be open to judgment.

We humans might say, in general, that violent, destructive thoughts are bad, while loving, constructive thoughts are good, which seems to match how a higher spirituality is said to bring peace and happiness instead of the warfare, anger, and sorrow of lower levels of perception. This sounds reasonable, but when we look closely at the universe, it seems to be built to a great degree on what we call violence, even though this violence can lead to positive results. For example, scientists think the universe itself started with an explosion so violent that regular atomic activity was impossible, and it expanded so fast that time had to rush along with it, all leading to our present existence.

Further, stars regularly sideswipe other stars, forcefully stripping off material they use to build solar systems that could have intelligent life, which could be where ours came from. Stars also can explode violently, but that action can release heavy atoms formed in their hot, high-pressure interiors, which is how our planet might have acquired the carbon and oxygen that form our bodies. Volcanoes can erupt with great destruction, but thereby bring forth new, mineral-rich earth that can give crops life and nutrition for us. Even when we just heat a can of soup for lunch, we cause a great agitation of particles crashing into each other, yet we accept this violence as normal.

Perhaps we need to hold off making judgments about good and bad until we understand a little more. The knowledge of ∞ God far surpasses ours, so we need to trust in it. We can only suggest the concept for our pondering that ∞ God has to have all the knowledge to be ∞ God—and that means *all*.

OMNIPOTENT

This term means that ∞ God is all-powerful. For too long it has been understood in very limited ways. Let us be blunt: All-powerful refers to having *all* of the power. Period. It does not mean just some of it, or sharing it with equally powerful beings, or having it apply in just certain locations or in certain situations or even just on this Earth. It means there can be no other being with the power of opposition to ∞ God in any way anywhere, since everything is interconnected.

Knowing something of the relationship of this Earth with just our solar system, not to mention our whole galaxy, there cannot be a god of only this Earth, with powers that just affect us. Instead, a little contemplation might suggest there is just ∞ God with the power to keep all the billions of stars and the masses of matter in the billions of galaxies of our universe in proper functioning order, and this is only the materialistic part. There are also conception, creation, consciousness, and thought on scales we can only imagine. We might meditate on the realization that there must be no other power existing beside that of ∞ God.

More than this, omnipotence also carries the power to keep all the vast numbers of tiny subatomic entities on this Earth functioning in perfect balance in exactly the same ways for all the eternities. If not under control by a being that always functions perfectly, everything would either fly apart, change character, or change location—and be out of control.

For example, since the atomic bomb has shown the immense power contained in a few rocks, imagine how much power is contained in all the rocks on Earth, which remains latent for the moment. All that power must be of ∞ God if ∞ God is omnipotent.

All atoms have nuclei of protons carrying like charge and are held together by what is called the strong force that keeps them from flying apart and wreaking havoc. And there is another called the weak force that allows some particles to decay. It is what makes the sun shine as the sun's hydrogen fuses into helium, releasing great energy. There are the vast numbers of electromagnetic forces involved in relationships and reactions throughout the universe, as well as inside the atom. And there is the force of gravity, which seems to take one form in the subatomic world and another in dealing with the enormous bodies of the universe. All these forces are in addition to the materialistic aspects we saw earlier. So, all the power to create and control everything everywhere needs to be of ∞ God through omnipotence.

We noted earlier that the concept of omniscience includes knowing all thoughts of all thinking entities everywhere. Now we might contemplate the idea that ∞ God, to be omnipotent, might need to actually be both the brain material, which includes the neural pathways, and also the sparks of thought along those pathways, as well as the consciousness or understanding of those thoughts. So we can see how we might receive spiritual intuitions once we stop blocking their flow by our individual thoughts of self-importance and ego.

All thoughts seem to be created as part of the allness of ∞ God, and we have innumerable paths we can take in our daily choices, including turning inward to thoughts of ourselves and our egos, or turning outward to spirituality and reception of spiritual intuition. The knowledge is available if we open ourselves to it. It is all ∞ God.

We might contemplate that ∞ God also functions as the bacteria, microbes, viruses, herbs, homeopathies, drugs, and all other phenomena that can both heal and destroy. All aspects of power are of ∞ God, and their wide variety is in the allness. How they are used brings us to the fringes of the meaningless question, "Why?" Let's just suggest that they are part of the complex interactions contained in life itself. The same can be said for the powers some living beings have to heal or eradicate each other.

The key thing to remember is that, since energy cannot be created or destroyed, the true essences of lives cannot be destroyed, only changed. There is a field of life that we can only dimly comprehend. Everything is interwoven and complex, and we limited humans need to open ourselves up more to the field through spirituality.

Perhaps it would make things easier if we saw this power or omnipotence of ∞ God as a field of strength that is motionless, quiet, self-sustaining (remembering that one Hebrew word for God means "The Self-Existent One"), constant and everlasting, an ambience rather than an action. It does not need to actually do anything because its strength is absolute. There is no power of which ∞ God is not the source and the totality. With that kind of power, everything just exists within Its field. Conversely, in the concept of force, there is compulsion, a movement, and a resultant opposition.

With power, there is none of this. It is a totality within which everything functions.

This view of ∞ God in total control of every aspect of the universe may not match the customary view of a comforting father figure, or a warrior chieftain leading the way in battle, or a judge to whom we plead for mercy. We will look at personification later. Here, we can just become aware of a power far greater than is often imagined, a different concept of the spiritual nature of the universe, an awareness that can be the key to our enlightenment.

OMNIPRESENT

Omnipresence is another word that must be used in a limitless sense. This can be a tough concept to grasp, but it is basic for comprehending ∞ God. The term suggests that ∞ God must be present everywhere, not only throughout space but in every atom, molecule, rock, tree, flower, person, meteor, planet, moon, star, galaxy, and universe that exists or ever will exist, and must be there completely, not just partially. That means being in the basic building blocks of the universe that we will look at shortly.

So ∞ God cannot be just nearby or a physical entity being represented by a spiritual aspect, because those would imply duality, not oneness, and would indicate there is a place where ∞ God isn't. This suggests that ∞ God needs to be the basis and fabric of everything, to be all there is. There must not be anything that is not ∞ God. Now, there are those who will laugh at this, thinking it is like the ancients who worshipped the sun, rain, lightning, or various animals as though they were gods. Nope. This is just becoming aware of true spirituality as the basis of creation, the spirituality of the one ∞ God.

Let us look more closely at that idea of duality. Over the generations, people have had the idea that we are "down here" while Deity is "up there." We also have had the idea that we were made as imperfect beings by the same Deity that will punish us severely for those imperfections if we do not find the vague path to overcome them and rise to rejoin that Deity in a heaven of perfect happiness forever. This concept is called "duality," and is one of the most difficult problems to overcome in gaining spiritual awareness. Let us think of it this way: Acceptance of the concept that ∞ God is all, being the sum total of everything that exists, gets rid of duality. There can be no separation of humankind from ∞ God in a total oneness because ∞ God is the essence of everything. So humans cannot be considered separated to live "down here" because ∞ God is present in them.

Likewise, humankind cannot be evil since ∞ God is its essence. There are consequences to actions, of course, and there are contrasts, which are just a part of the oneness, but evil, meaning opposition to ∞ God, is just a human judgment with almost as many opinions about it as there are people. It cannot exist in our new concepts.

Therefore, it is worthy to contemplate omnipresence as recognizing the oneness of ∞ God with all creation, being the fabric and completeness of all that is. If there is no thought that is not of ∞ God, nor any power that is not of ∞ God, then there can be no place without the presence of ∞ God for that power or those thoughts to operate. If there is oneness, It must be complete. There can be no place to which ∞ God only sends a representative, because ∞ God must be the complete power in every place, a totality. It is enlightening to contemplate that.

So, we have now taken literally and completely the three words that have been used lightly in the past by monotheists to describe their views of God. Obviously, the religious history of this world shows these the words have not been taken seriously enough, so just applying the thoughts we have seen so far could alter human views in a big way.

But we have many more advances that have been made in this world that can amplify our awareness even further, and one of them concerns energy, so we will consider that next.

Bringing the Awareness into Focus for Chapter 2

- Omniscient could mean knowing every detail of the universe, including the thoughts of sentient beings, as well as being the Creator of everything, since being something is the only way to really understand it.
- Omnipotent can refer to having all the power and control with no opposing force possible.
- Omnipresent can refer to existing everywhere as part of all entities, including living beings.

CHAPTER 3

Energy

The concept of energy is absolutely basic to an understanding of the universe that is ∞God according to Om³. There are many types of energy, which we will not go into here, but we do need to see where they come from and how they relate to us. We will not go very far into science, but our 21st century knowledge can give us a greater view of ∞God and energy than has been recognized thus far.

We are accustomed to referring to carbon and hydrogen as physical elements. And we are accustomed to speaking of chairs and rocks as physical things. We touch them, manipulate them, measure their density, and accept the concept that everything tangible has form and substance—and can be defined as matter.

But let's take a closer look at a wooden board: What is its main constituent? Space! A hydrogen atom, for example, consists of one proton and one electron. If we were to enlarge that proton to the size of a small marble, its electron would be the size of a speck of dust, orbiting it 150 feet away.

To picture this, if we were to place that marble on the fifteenth floor of a thirty-story building (thus imperceptible from the ground), the electron would orbit from the ground to the top of the building, totally invisible. And that is just a two-dimensional view. In three dimensions, the electron makes a shell around the marble. Other atoms are similar.

What is between them? A vast amount of space, at first glance, and also a lot of energy. But that proton and even that electron are not the smallest things in that board.

Going smaller than protons, we find hadrons. They, in turn, are made up of even smaller particles called quarks, which are held together by what is called the strong force. They have various properties, such as charge, mass, and spin. Their most obvious forms are protons (made up of two up quarks and one down quark) and neutrons (two down and one up). There are many more particles in the mix, of course, such as nutrinos, gluons, taus, muons, (and maybe even morons here and there). They are all arranged into family patterns when measured by mass and are controlled by the four basic forces we have identified in nature so far: the strong force, which keeps all the + charge protons tightly bound together in the nucleus of the atom instead of letting them repel each other; the weak force, which allows certain atoms to decay; electromagnetism, which comprises most of the things we deal with daily; and gravity, which is still not well understood.

By the way, there is work being done on recognizing a fifth force, a tiny one that could, nevertheless, possibly unite the other four. Some spiritual people, of course, suggest another overall power that might be seen to unite everything already: ∞ God.

We should note that all the vast quantities of these energies are kept in delicate balance. Any unplanned changes in the masses of the particles or the strengths of the forces that control them, no matter how slight, would create chaos in the universe as we know it. Not only is there an intelligent orderliness that random grouping might not have, but complete randomness would allow these energies to change constantly in unpredictable ways, but they do not, which might indicate a spiritual Intelligence behind them.

Quarks seem to be the smallest particles to experience all those four fundamental forces, so they might seem to be the smallest and most complete particles of all, but the question can still be asked: What makes up a quark?

There is one strong theory (backed by lots of research and successful experiments) that many scientists feel answers this. It gives the promise of uniting the three (and different, oddly enough) systems of physics (the Einsteinian physics of outer space, the Newtonian physics of our earthly world, and the subatomic world of quantum physics) into the one complete "Theory of Everything" that Einstein searched for the last thirty years of his life.

It is actually implicit in his most famous equation: $E=mc^2$, where E=energy; m=mass; and c=speed of light. Since c is just a constant, the equation really says that mass=energy. We may look at a rock or a star and think of them as material things that have mass, but actually they are just energy.

Everything around us and in the universe is pulsating energy. How can this be?

According to the string theory, all these sub-atomic particles are made up of ultra-tiny loops that physicists call "strings," entities that vibrate. Their size is far too small to be seen or accurately measured at the moment.

They do not break down any further because the key is not in the strings themselves but in their vibrations. The different frequencies of their vibrations produce the different elements we experience as carbon or iron or oxygen. So, instead of quarks, protons, atoms, molecules, bacteria, plants, rocks, animals, trees, planets, stars, and all the rest being made of different materials, they are all made of the *same stuff,* of these strings, which are *all identical,* and which vary from each other only by variations in their vibrations, vibrations that seem to give physical objects their individualities and existences. There is no mass to these strings because mass= energy. So these vibrations are all energy, and, therefore, all is energy, either in material form or in forces.

Since we have already seen the suggestion that ∞ God is all there is, this means that ∞ God includes energy. Of course, ∞ God is much more, as we will quickly see, but at the least, ∞ God is energy. We will see how this can be so later on when we look at the concept of personification.

So, since everything that seems to be physical is based on the vibrating energy of strings, and since energy is all there is, as we saw in Einstein's equation, this raises an interesting question: If there is nothing more fundamental than these strings, what is it that keeps the strings themselves vibrating in these exact patterns continually with no variations throughout the generations? What is more basic than they are?

Maybe it is ∞ God.

The scientific fact is that all four known forces we examined earlier use messenger particles to ensure obedience: Electromagnetism uses photons, gravity uses gravitons (not yet seen), the strong force uses gluons (excellent name), and the weak force uses w and z particles. If ∞ God is all there is, these messengers must be part of ∞ God also, and so "things" are made up of strings and forces much like how the tree we saw earlier is made of strings and forces that make up both its seeming form and also the special power that gives it life.

So ∞God needs to be, at least, everything that is, as well as the power that keeps it all functioning.

Now we can see how there is no dualism, with ∞ God separate from people and everything else, a Being that just moves objects about. Rather, ∞ God seems to be the essence of the universe and the basis of everything that seems to exist in it through being omniscient, omnipotent, and omnipresent, as well as the power that keeps it running smoothly and even gives it life.

This leads to a fascinating thought. One of the great questions pondered throughout the ages is: What is life? One simple answer could be that it is the generation of frequencies that animate something rather than just form it.

The tree we saw earlier can be a living thing, with branches and leaves, but when its life force generator stops, the leaves and branches, although still there for a while, start a transformation. The vibrations of their strings keep them as recognizable forms for a time, but then they begin to decay, fungi move in, and soon they change into other materials or energy types and furnish sustenance and life force for other trees. Their strings change vibrational patterns and frequencies when the life force generator is removed. So ∞ God is their essence but also, apparently, their life force producer.

Thus ∞ God may be the spark that can give life and animation to the objects that are destined to have it, such as humans. Does this mean rocks and stars do not get this life force?

Well, experiments with firing photons, the smallest particles of light, through a single slit in a barrier show that they make a round particle pattern on a screen, whereas when a second slit is opened, they make a wave or interference pattern on the screen, much like the interfering wave patterns from dropping two stones into a pond at the same time. This happens even when the photons are fired one at a time, so there can be no interference. In some ways, they seem to show a decision-making intelligence in varying their patterns in case of possible interference.

We know, also, that individual cells in our bodies carry on intelligent functions apart from messages received from the brain. Perhaps the animating power is present in different ways in seemingly inert objects. This idea opens us to a whole new world of the totality of ∞ God and of the definition of life.

And if these things are true, what other powers does ∞ God have? In what other dimensions?

We note that one interesting aspect of the string theory is that its equations only work in nine dimensions rather than our usual three. Adding the dimension of time makes ten. And since there are at least five different string theories, scientific thought found it necessary to add one more dimension to unite them all, creating the superstring theory.

Thus, we are talking about a universe of at least eleven dimensions (some scientists add more), which we, as yet, cannot visualize. Some scientists have tried to picture them as tiny, curled up spheres at every point along the normal dimensions, and some math models seem to confirm this, but there is another way to think of them.

Suppose you are standing next to a friend. You can see the three basic physical dimensions and, when you note the time of day, you see four. However, your friend is complex and may have three dimensions of emotions. You can't see them, but they are right there in front of you. And there might be three intellectual dimensions you cannot see, yet all these added dimensions give a more complete and in-depth knowledge of the person than just the physical. This might be approaching a more ∞ God-like view.

So the dimensions of the strings might lead to a new awareness necessary for an appreciation of ∞ God. Remember how we saw that the only way to really understand something is to actually *be* it? Humans as yet do not have knowledge of the totality of a person the way ∞ God has by virtue of actually being the person in all the various dimensions of Om^3.

Let us see one way this might be so. String theory now indicates that some strings are open (meaning that the loose ends are free) and some are closed in a complete loop. The ends of the open strings are actually limited by or even fastened to the multi-dimensional frame or "brane" in which they exist. Therefore, they can move around inside their branes but not move outside.

Closed strings are independent, not limited by branes, and so can move around various dimensions. It turns out that photons, the smallest particles of light and the units by which we visually sense everything, are open strings, and thus are contained within this three-dimensional world or brane in which we all seem to exist.

This type of world is all we can see by means of the light photons around us. This means that they not only render this brane invisible to us (since they can travel anywhere inside it and there is no contrast by which we can distinguish it, much like a whiteout in a snowstorm), but also that they cannot travel to any other dimensions, and so we cannot see or measure those other dimensions.

These might be located right next to us, as we

have already realized, but we cannot detect them. However, we can grasp the concept of them in our thoughts, so thoughts might be closed strings, able to travel anywhere, and this is a critical part of our ability to overcome limits and to soar free.

Now, only one of the particles scientists know of so far is made of closed-loop strings, and that is the graviton, able to travel anywhere. The graviton seems also to be an attractive force, so it could be that our thoughts are related to gravitons and have an attractive force. Many people say that the things you think are attracted to you, and if you want good things in life, just set your intentions on them and they will have the ability and openness to flow to you.

Perhaps the graviton plays a role in this. After all, in our minds we can conceive many things that we cannot see, which act forms a big part of artistic creativity. If we think in terms of limitlessness, we might be able to accomplish the same things metaphysically. It is worthy of contemplation.

All of this means we humans might be eleven-dimensional entities, of far greater complexity than we or even scientific theory can picture at the moment, so that most of our worrying about such problems as what will happen to us after death is moot because we cannot fathom the totality of who we really are right now, except to be aware that we are, and always will be, of ∞ God, seeing our true selves only when our earthly egos fall away and stop blocking the spiritual.

After all, if we are multi-dimensional, then the universe might also be multi-dimensional. The fact that the body we seem to occupy in this particular universe ceases to function does not necessarily mean that we have ceased in any other universe. Also, since we do not know most of our dimensions here, how can we insist on keeping these particular ones after we move on? Maybe there really are better ones awaiting us.

Only a superior Intelligence that is omniscient, omnipotent, and omnipresent can know and control all of this in a wholeness and completeness that includes us in the totality of energy. Since there is nothing existing but energy and since, therefore, we are energy and a part of the whole, we have nothing to fear. Great things await.

Bringing the Awareness into Focus for Chapter 3

- The smallest indivisible aspects of everything in the universe are vibrating entities called strings, which are all alike and which give different characteristics to matter through their varieties of vibrations.

- Everything that exists is just vibrating energy, operating in eleven dimensions.

- The only power more fundamental than the strings would be the intelligence that directs and controls them, which can be thought of as ∞ God.

CHAPTER 4

Vibrations & Frequencies

Let us look a little more at the role of vibrations in all this. We have seen Einstein's famous equation, $E=mc^2$. It is said that if you managed to squeeze all the vast amounts of actual matter in the universe as tightly together as possible, it wouldn't fill a thimble. There is no matter because it is all energy.

But there is another equation similar to Einstein's, although much less known: $E=h\nu$. E, again, equals energy, but h=Planck's constant (which is a tiny number and doesn't concern us here), and ν is the Greek letter nu (N is the capital letter, ν is the lowercase one) which equals frequencies, not just vibrations as the ν seems to indicate. So, energy equals frequency of vibrations, and energy also equals mass, so mass equals frequency of vibrations. This is to be expected because energy implies movement.

Energy is defined as the capacity for doing work, and most work requires motion. A rock may seem to sit there inert, without any movement, but we know it is filled with atomic activity in furious motion, and if all the energy in it were released, there would be an immense explosion. It is also made of atoms which are made of strings that, themselves, are composed of nothing but energy. And these strings are vibrating at certain frequencies that determine the types of matter or energy that make up the rock. So frequencies are involved all the time in making distinctive entities.

To put it simply, the higher the frequency of vibrations, the greater the energy. And the greater the mass, the greater the energy contained in it.

Let's see how guitar strings illustrate some important thoughts about vibrations. Guitar strings are tuned E-A-D-G-B-E, from the bottom up. Now let us firmly pluck the open higher E, and then stop it. The sound will continue. Do it again and again, and it will keep ringing. What could be making the tone if you have stopped the string? Do it again and check the bottom E and you will find it is doing the vibrating. Why? Because it is also tuned to E, albeit two octaves lower. Being tuned in sync, it develops sympathetic resonance and vibrates along with the top string being touched only by the vibrations through the air and from the sounding board.

Does that sound like the way people can vibrate in sync with others on their wavelengths?

Let us ponder a little more on that. We note that the lower string is not vibrating at its own basic low frequency but has subdivided itself into smaller segments that vibrate at the same pitch as the higher string. We can actually see the sections vibrate. So the induced string matches the exact pitch of the inducing string. The spiritual implications are clear: If we are spiritually in tune with ∞ God, we can vibrate at the same spiritual pitch;

Chapter 4: VIBRATIONS & FREQUENCIES

not at just our version of it (our own lower one) but at the correct higher pitch, and will therefore represent that same level of energy.

Going back to the guitar, we can go one step further. When we pluck the high E and stop it, and then also stop the low E from vibrating, the sound *still* goes on, but softer. Where is it now? It is in the fifth string, tuned to A, which is related to E harmonically, and so on it goes. Being in tune in the first place is the key (that's a musical joke), but even being related harmonically carries a relationship. So, if we are in tune with something (high or low), its vibrations can easily be induced in us. If we humans are in tune with energetic people around us, we can find ourselves vibrating at their levels. The same applies to those around us at lower vibrations. We can tune ourselves as we choose, of course, and that reflects who we are. If we tune ourselves to the level of spiritual vibrations, those can be induced in us. Our choice. Vibrations constitute all things, and we are our vibrations. We can choose our resonance.

Here is an interesting observation, whose meaning will become clearer later. If we take a glass goblet, ascertain its pitch, and sing that exact pitch in a strong voice, the goblet will begin to vibrate and may even shatter because it is too stiff and brittle to absorb the vibrations.

Resiliency and flexibility are the important things here, which we will see later when we take a quick look at the quantum.

Now, of course, these are just slow-moving sound waves traveling through air, so sounds require a medium and are of no use in space. Electromagnetic entities vibrate at much higher frequencies, but similar principles apply. Much as vibrating strings induce harmonic resonance that causes other strings to vibrate, producing notes, electromagnetic entities induce resonance in other particles through messenger particles, producing effects. We are familiar with the electromagnetic spectrum, which exists throughout space, and in which infrared, radio, ultraviolet, even light itself, and other waves and particles vary from each other by their frequencies of vibrations.

Well, the vibrations of ∞ God cover the whole gamut since ∞ God is all energy levels in all the matter of the universe and can induce other frequencies at various harmonic levels to all the matter in the universe, thus keeping everything steady. This is part of the constant creativity of ∞ God. But to do so involves influencing a vast number of strings in their different forms to keep them all vibrating in their exact patterns so that materials keep their same forms. A physical force might have trouble doing that. This could indicate a superior intelligence guiding it all. Since these frequencies can affect others through resonance, a superior power can form resonance at various levels in anything. This is tapping into Universal Mind to create our total reality.

Let us look at another aspect of this. We know particles in the electromagnetic field that surrounds us are constantly popping up into existence and affecting other particles before dropping back into the soup, as it were. One effect particles have on one another is spin. All particles have spin in different forms and, indeed, are defined by it. Well, it has been shown that one particle can affect the spin of another at a speed far faster than the speed of light, the highest speed known. In fact, they can be considered to interact simultaneously even though relatively far apart.

Some mathematicians have even tried to show that there is a speed greater than that of light, which Einstein declared impossible. There is an easier solution: the awareness that everything is ∞ God. If all is of one body, then there can definitely be interactions happening at the same instant, and different frequencies can be carried on simultaneously, much like a referee raising both arms simultaneously to signal a touchdown, or all of a cat's fur standing up at the same time when a dog approaches.

Let us look again at the formula $E=hv$, and note again that as vibrations increase, energy increases. When we bring a burning candle near a match head, the match will burst into flame from the radiated or induced heat that increases molecular activity in it to the point of ignition. A rock may contain great internal atomic activity to maintain its form as a rock; without induced heat it lies there inert with no discernible activity. A radioactive rock may seem to be lying there inert as well, but it is exerting effects on its surroundings through possibly destructive radiation. Flowing molten lava, though, shows great activity and possible destructive effects on its surroundings.

The difference among them is potential versus kinetic energy. The regular rock has enough potential energy for a huge atomic explosion, but it remains potential until stimulated. The molten lava exhibits great kinetic energy, while the radioactive rock actually has both. Created beings have the same energy.

Since ∞ God is all frequencies, humans can tap into these through induction and resonance, if they are tuned to the proper frequency area to start with. The candle can ignite the match head but cannot ignite a metal nail head. Just as with the audience we discussed in Chapter 1, the person who is alert, receptive, and tuned into the music will have a fine experience, whereas the sleeping person will assume nothing is happening. Spiritual enlightenment is all around, but we have to tune into it.

Is there a God frequency for this tuning in? There have been candidates but no conclusive evidence. It is far more likely that a wide range of frequencies is employed, from the lowest to the highest. We note that higher frequencies seem to generate constructive or creative activity, but they can also be destructive to the unprepared. The goblet shatters. We also remember that, as temperatures drop, vibrational activity also drops, which can produce quiet benefits unless it drops to zero degrees Kelvin, where everything stops.

Let us set up a heat source, a glass of ice water, and a bridge between them. Will the heat flow to the cold, or will the cold flow to the heat? Well, cold is just the absence of heat, so the high-frequency heat will go to the low-frequency cold, and heat's faster molecular activity will warm things up a little.

We noted earlier that such emotions as anger, hate, and worry are low-vibration or destructive or cold traits, but they can have little effect unless other people tune into them. And their vibrations can be raised, if they are willing, by people of a higher tuning. Love, kindness, and spirituality are considered high-vibration, constructive, warm traits, but they can also be rejected by the person who is not ready or receptive. We note that some people do quite well in situations of high activity, while others need a lower-pitched atmosphere to be comfortable. It is all ∞ God.

We also note that our bodies are made up of a great number of different entities, all vibrating at different frequencies. Each atom of iron in our cells, for example, has a different frequency from the magnesium atoms in the same cell.

Adding up all the different frequencies in our bodies can give quite a mixture that can easily have an effect on our overall personal radiation. Some people have more or less of something than the next person, and they vibrate and respond differently. Since ∞ God is in all frequencies and can induce enlightenment at any level, the highest is not necessarily the best in all instances for people to relate to and help one another.

Finally, scientists have discovered the Higgs Field, a non-zero value field existing throughout the universe that adds mass to particles if they are accelerating through it. Since mass=energy, particle acceleration therefore increases energy, whereas just drifting along doesn't. It seems that higher energy can, indeed, be gained by those who actively seek it. It depends on how we tune ourselves.

So, like the volunteer who goes into a state prison increases the spiritual levels of the inmates, or the nun working among the poor and sick raises them in health and hope, all of us can reach out to help increase the growth of other souls using spiritual harmonies. Just like children might not identify with a parent who achieves great fame and power in the world, but do identify with the parent who takes care of them and plays with them, we don't have to show the highest levels of spirituality. We grow continually as we help others at various levels to find greater awareness of ∞ God.

But now comes the wrench in the works: To get a true 21st century view, we have to look at the world of the quantum. Again, we are not going too deep, but the principles are vital to our spiritual growth.

Bringing the Awareness into Focus
for Chapter 4

- The higher the vibrations, the greater their energy, and since vibrations can be induced in other entities, allowing them to vibrate at the levels to which they are tuned, thinking beings can decide their own levels and strengths of energy.

- Instant interaction between entities often occurs, suggesting that everything is part of one great being, which can be thought of as ∞ God.

- The Higgs Field suggests that higher energy levels can be attained by those who actively seek them rather than just drift along.

CHAPTER 5

The Quantum

Before we get too comfortable in a fixed, straight-out view of ∞ God, we need to note the subatomic world called the quantum, and we will learn some amazing things about ∞ God and about ourselves from it. This knowledge is vital to our search.

Chapter 5: THE QUANTUM

The word comes from the scientific discovery that energy at subatomic levels is not released evenly, as we might expect, but in packets called quanta. This realization resolved a great many puzzles that had obstructed scientists as they tried to understand the subatomic world using conventional physics.

The quantum is its own world, and we remember that we are faced with three distinct systems of physics: the Newtonian system that works in our world; the Einsteinian system that only works in outer space; and the quantum, which only works in its subatomic world. They are all different, and problems in one cannot be solved using the rules or equations of the others. Einstein and others have worked for many years to unify them into one complete "Theory of Everything," and it hasn't happened yet.

In earthly or Newtonian physics, things tend to work out in precise, balanced forms. We have a formula, we plug in our numbers, we get a result. If we or anyone else make use of the same formulas and numbers, we all get the same results. Well and good.

But in the quantum, there is only a probability that a result will occur in a certain way, and the results can be different for different experimenters. Let us say that an electron circling a nucleus decides to jump from its shell of orbit to another shell, which gives us our first hint that things are different in this new world: We do not know why it does that. And then we run into the role that probability plays.

Let us make up some numbers to show this. Assume that the electron can only jump to shells A, B, or C because of electrical factors. It may have only a thirty percent probability of jumping to orbit A, thirty percent to B, and forty percent to C. That is as close as we can get. This means that, if we create an equation that picks A, we have only a thirty percent chance of being correct. If our equation picks C, our chance of being correct only goes to forty percent. The best equations in quantum mechanics are only forty percent accurate. But there are enough of them that they are surprisingly correct.

There is another element of this that does affect you and me continually. Before the electron actually jumps, it tries out each possible orbit first. It seems to fuzzy itself out over all three orbits at the same time, therefore being in three places at once, in a cloud that is called a wave of probabilities, and then it chooses one and jumps to it in what is called a collapse into a particle form. In many instances, such as light, it can exist as both wave and particle simultaneously, and evidence is now mounting that most different phenomena can exist in both states, which makes the process of understanding ∞ God from the physical universe even harder. It seems to suggest that aspects of ourselves can also exist in different states at the same time. We are not just one, but many all at once. We recall that the strings that constitute us and everything else operate in many more dimensions than we can presently understand, so this is to be expected.

And this concept of how everything can be both wave and particle, and can collapse in different ways, means that each piece of each entity constitutes a field, rather than a spot. Fields contain movement. So everything everywhere is a vast pattern of fields, changing, collapsing, interacting, and influencing each other. And of great interest to us is that we living beings contain vast numbers of such fields, all doing the same things, and possibly our thoughts are also fields, influencing everything else in the universe.

We can, then, affect the universe with our thoughts and consciousnesses, as mystics have been saying all along. Indeed, thinking and consciousness are necessary to existence. The universe is apparently not just lumps of rocks whirling around, but is interactive, thoughtful, and open to many interpretations, and all of it seems to be ∞ God.

Notice how Chinese medicine has based itself on how chi, the life force, flows along certain meridians in the body, showing how blockage of this flow tends to bring on illnesses. This might lead us to see how flowing and movement can therefore be beneficial in universal interactions, with blockage having the opposite effect.

We remember how the Higgs Field gives mass to accelerating particles, not idle ones, and we note that absolute zero temperature would lead to a cessation of all movement, if it could be reached. But the universe maintains a temperature throughout itself a little bit above that, so there is always movement. We might, therefore, glimpse the concept that more growth and increased energies are beneficial in our constantly growing and evolving universe, as we see in the Big Bang Theory. It is interesting that the universe is not only still expanding from the point of that first explosion but actually seems to be gaining speed, which was not expected in early observations. Movement is vital, in the original meaning of the word "quicken," referring to life.

But there is more, and the spiritual aspect is also strong here. We are unclear on all the things that cause a wave to collapse into particle form, but one way is for the wave to be observed or measured. Now, there is little uniformity in this: If you observe or measure it, the collapse may be into this form here, whereas if I do it, it might be into that form there, and if no one does it, the collapse might be totally different. So you and I are each creating different realities out of the same situation.

The spiritual implications are clear in that none of us is right or wrong or any less than each other, but that we all create our own spiritual reality. This leads to great variety in the world and in the universe, but it is all one in ∞ God. Everyone needs to be respected for doing individual things, so we operate in a vagueness of individualities. Getting a handle on what the universe/∞ God really are can get increasingly difficult as we grow in knowledge and awareness.

In fact, there is some scientific speculation about the existence of multiple universes. If the possibilities of a wave finally collapse into just one particle form, starting a chain of events that domino into a particular universe, what happens to the other possibilities in the cloud? Do they collapse into other particle forms, thus creating other universes? It is worthy of thought.

And the final blow is the famous Heisenberg Uncertainty Principle. Let me illustrate it.

If I want to send a helicopter to a ship at sea, I need to know two things about the ship: its location and its velocity, which includes both its speed and direction. If I know only its position and I send the helicopter there, it will probably find nothing because the ship will have moved. If I know only its velocity, I have no idea where to begin plotting its course. But if I know where it is right now as well as its speed and direction, I can send the helicopter to the correct place to intercept it.

The same goes for a particle: To work with it, I need to know its location and its velocity. But in the quantum, as part of the world of uncertainty, we have the Heisenberg Principle, which states that the more I know about a particle's location, the less I know of its velocity, and vice versa. This is not the fault of the instruments or of the physicists, but is just built into the system. We simply cannot know both aspects of the particle completely—and never will be able to. It is closed to us. So there is no way we can know enough to limit or define ∞ God with our human thinking.

Even further, we remember from earlier that scientists now suspect that just about all things—electrons, quarks, protons, and all else—are waves as well as particles and, therefore, have probabilities. And the math involved is staggering. An electron's wave, for example, has the chance of collapsing in places throughout the universe, as well as in the shells we are accustomed to. The chances of it doing so are next to nothing, but there are so many chances that they have to be taken into account, and the math to do that is extremely complex; further, we would still be dealing only in probabilities. The same goes for all the different ways people think and act, and yet all are of the totality of ∞ God.

All this just reenforces the nagging suspicion that we can never know much about ∞ God or other people. However, just like physicists in the quantum who don't worry about their limitations and just keep calculating and getting results anyway, we can take our knowledge as far as possible and use it to better our lives and the life of the whole planet.

But like the scientists, we cannot do this just with data from the past. We need to use our 21st century knowledge and data as enlightened people to advance our spiritual awarenesses, which is the basic aim of this book.

By heightening our spiritual awareness, we can activate more elements of our higher minds, such as intuition, through which we can receive insights directly from the source to which we are attuned as mystics, which is another aim of our time together here.

Bringing the Awareness into Focus for Chapter 5

- The subatomic quantum world has its own system of physics based on probabilities instead of certainties. It functions well in dimensions we don't understand, but which are part of the great Intelligence of the universe.

- All things exist as clouds of possibilities that can collapse into different specific forms for different observers, explaining why we are all so different from each other.

- The Heisenberg Principle shows how humans can never know all the aspects of the universe, thus strengthening dependence on individual revelations from ∞ God.

CHAPTER 6

Personification

This is a big sticking point.

We humans tend to personify things. A ship is "she," for example, and a motorcycle is "he." We give names to hurricanes and speak of them by gender. We enjoy watching animals acting like people.

In the same manner, many humans tend to personify God according to their own understandings: some as a fierce judge, some as a loving father, some as a warrior leading troops into battle, some as a dazzling figure on a throne surrounded by angels. When depicted in art or movies, God can take the form of a human, an intense light, a whirlwind, or even be invisible but still with a voice. Some of us just want the caring embrace of a parent to extend to our Deity.

The concept of ∞ God as the essence and motivating power behind the universe and all creation with no human body or human characteristics can be difficult to visualize or appreciate with our present egos. But we now realize that we and everything else are just energy, so there might be less problem now with extending that concept to Deity.

Still, let us look at some astronomy first and then some physics to get a better perspective.

As we touched on in Chapter 1, we live on a modest planet, circling a medium star, off to one side in a trailing arm of a galaxy containing billions of such stars, at least millions of which probably have planets at the proper distance from their star to allow development of intelligent life of various forms. Then, our huge galaxy, the Milky Way, is lost among billions of other such galaxies, each with billions of stars and plenty of possible worlds capable of having all sorts of intelligent beings. Plus every bit of that massive quantity out there possibly has the same quantum complexity throughout that we have. And there is every possibility that there are multitudes of different systems of physics out there leading to entities we cannot even imagine.

And yet we assume that the God that is the motivating power behind all of this massiveness needs to look like us and act like us and even have some of our human weaknesses. Isn't that maybe too much personification?

Now let us use physics and anatomy to see something else. When we "see" something, light photons from a radiating source reflect from it and strike our eyes, causing them to send messages along neural pathways to our brains where they are interpreted as the image of what is out there. So when we see something, we are dealing only with electrochemical reactions and with vibrations at different frequencies. We are not actually experiencing anything directly, much as how movies and videos on our TV sets or computers seem real but are only electromagnetic signals relating to a reality existing elsewhere. When people hallucinate, those visions seem just as real, even though there's nothing there. When we have a thought or a memory, we are reacting to electrochemical impulses in the brain. When we have a vision, it's the same.

But these signals in the brain seem to be just physical and, as such, cannot account for our imaginations, creative thoughts, understandings, or even consciousness itself. All these are apparently aspects of our minds, which are independent of our brains and have their own energy fields. We can therefore suspect that our understandings could come directly from the energy of the Source as we saw earlier, the one Mind of the universe.

What part of us does the responding to the Source? No one knows. We do not know what life force is, what consciousness is, what the soul is. We do know that a living being functions so long as it has a living energy, a spark.

When that goes, the being is still there in its complexity for a while, but ceases to function and will probably soon decay and change into something else, as with the tree earlier. This animating life force is from the outside, something more basic than the strings that make up the physical form. We can call this life force one aspect of ∞ God.

This all takes some getting used to.

Can we, then, have visions? Of course. They are how each consciousness interprets certain neural-chemical impulses in our brains. Anciently, lightning caused fear, wonder, and worship. Today, those same strikes bring different understandings and emotions. The strikes have changed because our concepts of them have changed, and we see them more completely than did ancient people. It is each person's interpretation that is different.

Can we picture God as a father figure who loves us? As a judge who punishes us? As a king who grants the petitions of some but denies the requests of others? As a companion who walks with us? Of course we can. We just need to remember that these are all wave forms collapsing into particles that will be different for different people, as we saw in the quantum, and so we need to understand and allow for other people's interpretations.

We should not condemn because everything is just different forms of energy that are perceived in various ways by various brains which, themselves, are different forms of energy.

Well, what of the concepts that God is love, that the universe is filled with love, that love is the solution to all problems? We must note that the word "love" covers such a bewildering variety of emotions that it is difficult to define it properly. Types of love can include the bucolic love from afar of old courtly times; teenage infatuation; casual reactions on a date; the development of intense caring between an engaged pair; inflamed passions, including lust, over-possessiveness, and selfishness; the intense euphoria of newlyweds; the quiet, accepting feelings of a long-married elderly couple; the selfless giving of the altruist; the spirituality referred to in the Greek word agape; and so forth.

It should be added that the passions of love can be so unstable that they can change almost instantly to hatred or devastation. So using the word "love" can give rise to all sorts of misunderstandings.

It might be better to use the word in capital letters as an acronym meaning: Level Of Veritable Enlightenment. Since veritable means real or genuine, we might LOVE others as if we were enlightened already in this earthly existence, living a life of warmth, kindness, acceptance, caring, unity, appreciation, and a cherishing of all around us. We will then possibly realize that these are the attributes of an intensely spiritual life that will open us to a greater personal awareness of ∞ God. And awareness is the key. Since true LOVE consists of accepting and caring about each person, plant, rock, animal, and earthly feature exactly as it is by being aware of its spiritual essence, this elevation of consciousness can lead to spiritual peace and fulfillment through enlightenment or seeing more as spirituality sees.

So, do we have complete freedom of thought, total free will, to think as we choose? Or does ∞ God control our thoughts? Well, the randomness of the quantum world, the vast number of possibilities available in life, the personal particle collapses from waves of possibilities all seem to indicate that all ideas we might have already exist in ∞ God. And they are there for us to choose from freely while still being within ∞ God. Since ∞ God can also be known as Universal Mind, our minds form a part of that Mind and partake of the benefits of It in a subjective way, even experiencing the creativity of the ideas we conceive. But there is an aspect to this subjective creativity that needs to be considered.

People growing up or living in a particular religious or cultural environment generally tend to follow the practices of that environment because they know no others. As an example, a speaker on communications might go into the middle of an audience to hold up a picture so all can see it clearly and then go back up front to put a big version of it on an easel and ask audience members to describe what they see. Some will say that it is a picture of

Chapter 6: PERSONIFICATION

a young girl, while others will insist that it is an old witch.

Arguments can get quite heated, with people even going up to the picture and pointing out the lines of what they see. Gradually, it becomes apparent that the people in the front of the room see the girl while those in the back see the witch. What the speaker did, of course, while in the middle of the group, was show a distinct picture of a girl to the front half of the room, a distinct picture of a witch to the back half, and then put a composite of the two on the easel. People in the front and the back will see what the teacher trained them to see and will have trouble seeing something else even when it is pointed out to them.

So it may be hard for people to see religious beliefs beyond the ones they grew up with and are comfortable with. This is why we use the term ∞ God in this book to show a new view, different from that of the God of our past. So, maybe we will gain more freedom of thought by contemplating the new aspects of ∞ God hinted at in this book.

Of all these myriad beliefs in the world, which ones are correct? The answer still could be that everyone is on an individual life path, as we saw earlier, and waves of possibilities collapse differently for different observers, so there is no "correct."

This is all part of the complex creativity that is ∞ God. Humans deal in limitations constantly without even knowing it, and so breaking free from some of those limitations, opening our awarenesses to a bigger or even an unlimited view of ∞ God, might possibly lead to avoidance of some unspiritual ways in which people have treated each other in the past in the name of religion.

This is because spirituality and religion tend to be opposites; the first unlimited, the second constricted by required belief systems, practices, rituals, and group pressure. They both continue to function because they are part of the complex total creativity that is ∞ God. However, individuals can grow in spirituality by establishing their own ways of collapsing their waves of possibilities, taking different roles within spirituality.

Reading and pondering thoughts such as those in this book can start the process toward a different awareness of ∞ God.

Does ∞ God speak to people? Interesting question, because ∞ God *is* the people, their *essence*, which can be sensed when we open up awareness and sweep away the worldly blockages. Remember, how we choose what to listen to or how to interpret it is up to us in our vast array of choices, an array, however, often influenced by others, as we saw in the pictures of the witch and the girl earlier. People tend to create the God of their narrow choice until they become more aware of the totality of ∞ God, the Infinite Deity. Again, awareness is the key.

Here is another aspect. We humans consider ourselves to be distinct individuals, with our own bodies, personalities, egos, thoughts, and emotions, and we may want these to continue on forever because this is who we think we are, our identity. We may even force our beliefs on others, thinking we are right and they are wrong.

Let us remember that our bodies are only mixtures of vibrating frequencies. Thoughts are mental cognitions in vibrating brains traveling and branching along neural pathways. Attitudes are long-term thoughts. Emotions are psychological states brought on by the neurophysiological changes from these thoughts. And our personalities are the collections of all of these things that we use to identify ourselves to others as a package.

But these collections do not represent who we really are. Here is a concept to consider: perhaps our minds are vibrating energy fields themselves, with the energy coming either from our cells (since we remember that the cells carry on many functions uncontrolled by the brain) or even directly from ∞ God. We just use our brains to classify and use the information from our minds. If so, then, a mind field could be in contact with other energy fields, both nearby and at various distances, involved in receiving knowledge directly as a mystic does. So, at our core, we are ∞ God, Source of our energy.

The brain in meditation tends to chatter along, endlessly repeating old thoughts, having trouble staying in focus. But the mind, related to Universal Mind and seat of higher receptivity, including intuition, is different and could be open to direct revelation, showing that the universe might, as we mentioned before, be more philosophical, personal, and participatory than just mechanical since its waves of possibilities collapse in all kinds of ways.

For this to be seen, of course, requires a greater awareness than we limited humans can generally grasp. Yet it might be worth the effort to try.

When the body and brain are stilled in death, the mind or consciousness, which has been observed to continue on, using its own energy source, can expand unchecked, possibly locking on to other energy sources, becoming an eternal soul within the oneness of ∞ God.

What a stupendous concept: We are one in ∞ God! If we open our consciousnesses to an awareness of who we and all others really are, we can gain the enlightenment that we seek within what we can call Universal Spiritual Awareness. Let us finish here with a look at that.

Bringing the Awareness into Focus for Chapter 6

- Humans tend to personify ∞ God with human characteristics and limitations as they have been taught by their social environments, which are based on old knowledge.

- The Universal Intelligence can manifest Itself in human minds and emotions as a wide variety of characteristics and vivid experiences, since perceptions seem to be reality to the mind.

- Knowing that all is energy, it could be that humans are vibrating energy fields, the basis of which, when worldly self-identifications are stripped away, is ∞ God.

CHAPTER 7

Universal Spiritual Awareness

What do we do with all of this?
One way is to practice Universal Spiritual Awareness.

Chapter 7: UNIVERSAL SPIRITUAL AWARENESS

As we look again at the levels of consciousness of the concert goers in the first chapter, we note that the one seeming to get the most out of the performance is the one awake, alert, and actively participating in and appreciating the performance with both conscious awareness of what is happening and sensitivity to the deeper meaning of it. This sounds like an ideal state, so let us look into it further.

In an opera audience, we can focus on several who seem to be awake and alert. One may be interested mainly in the conductor, watching all the subtle ways he brings out his interpretation of the music. Another may be looking for the prettiest girl or handsomest man in the orchestra or on the stage to focus on. Another may be interested in following the musical line of just one instrument. Another may be watching the different singing techniques used. Another may be taking in the spectacle as a whole, enjoying the colors and movements. Another may be interested in the libretto, while another is distracted by nuance noises or coughing, thereby being annoyed and losing track of the music. Another may be comparing different aspects of the performance with the memory of a past one or a recording.

In all of these, there may be portions of awareness, but not a totality and, therefore, not a unity. But in the audience as a whole, all of these may be present in a group unified in their individualities. No one is right or wrong, just individuals in a unity situation. They can be seen as representing humanity, in a way.

So universal means everything joined together as one, a totality. It doesn't necessarily mean a blending in which everything just melts into a formless mess, but rather a collection of individuals as a group, respecting individuality. We remember that all things in the universe are made from the same strings that differ only in their vibrating energy, so we, the rocks, and the stars are all the same basically, and differ only in the roles assigned to us by vibrations in the creative energy that is ∞ God, since ∞ God is all there is. So we don't mean blending humans, trees, and rocks into a formless mass but, rather, rejoicing in the oneness we have as individuals in ∞ God.

We recall that we don't need to waste time striving to achieve the highest levels of vibrating energy because ∞ God is present in all levels, and we can keep in touch with creation through dealing with all

Chapter 7: UNIVERSAL SPIRITUAL AWARENESS

aspects of relationships, rather than isolating ourselves only at the highest. We remember that ∞ God is in illness and despair as well as in health and joy, in the low notes of the performance as well as in the high notes, so universal means being cognizant of it all. Universal, then, means all-encompassing.

Spirituality at its simplest refers to seeing the essence, the soul, along with the material or physical. But we can go farther with it. It can also mean seeing the totalities of things—their relationships to ∞ God, their symbolisms, their influences on others, their depths, their places and meanings in the universe. Becoming aware of the infinite variety of creation, we just deal with the vast variety of people and situations in our world, accepting and working with them, recognizing that ∞ God is the essence of them all, and learning to live in peace and happiness amongst them.

Awareness refers to the opening of consciousness to the realization that ∞ God is all there is, the essence of all that exists, and suggests that our highest goal in earthly life might be for us to draw together to recognize and respect this oneness and our individual roles in It.

Thus, Universal Spiritual Awareness joins all of us together in the presence of ∞ God at all levels. This, of course, has been the theme of this book from the beginning. So let us do it. Let us all draw together in a true Universal Spiritual Awareness, enjoying the peace, freedom, earthly happiness, spiritual joy, and confidence in the future that this brings.

Namaste.

About the Author

John Walker, *Ph.D., has been a university professor and administrator, secondary school educator, religious institute director, prison minister/teacher, Army officer, cryptanalyst at NSA, ham radio operator specializing in emergency communications, and life-long musician. He and his wife, Corky, also an educator, live in Southern California, with a family tree of descendants numbering more than sixty including spouses. He can be reached at:*

universalspiritualawareness@protonmail.com

Bibliography

Greene, Brian. 2003. *The Elegant Universe.* New York: Vintage Books.

Greene, Brian. 2011. *The Hidden Reality.* New York: Alfred A. Knopf.

Hawking, Stephen. 1996. *A Brief History of Time.* New York: Bantam Books.

Hawking, Stephen. 2010. *The Grand Design.* New York: Bantam Books.

Hawkins, Dr. David R. 2003. *I: Reality and Subjectivity.* Carlsbad, CA: Hay House.

Hunt, Valerie. 1996. *Infinite Mind.* Malibu, CA: Malibu Publishing.

Lipton, Bruce. 2005. *The Biology of Belief.* Santa Rosa, CA: Elite Books.

Murphy, Dr. Joseph. 1963. *The Power of Your Subconscious Mind.* Englewood Cliffs, NJ: Prentice Hall.

Peat, F. David. 1988. *Super Strings and the Search for the Theory of Everything.* Chicago: Contemporary Books.

Wolf, Fred Alan. 1988. *Parallel Universes.* New York: Simon and Schuster.

Zukav, Gary. 1979. *The Dancing Wu Li Masters.* New York: HarperCollins.

www.ingramcontent.com/pod-product-compliance
Lightning Source LLC
Chambersburg PA
CBHW070450050426
42451CB00015B/3422